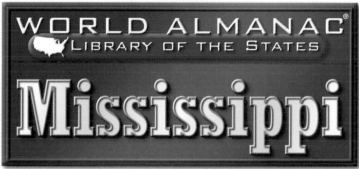

The Magnolia State

by Acton Figueroa

WORLD ALMANAC® LIBRARY

Please visit our web site at: **www.worldalmanaclibrary.com**
**For a free color catalog describing World Almanac® Library's list of high-quality books
and multimedia programs, call 1-800-848-2928 (USA) or 1-800-387-3178 (Canada).
World Almanac® Library's fax: (414) 332-3567.**

Library of Congress Cataloging-in-Publication Data available upon request
from publisher. Fax (414) 336-0157 for the attention of the Publishing
Records Department.

ISBN 0-8368-5152-8 (lib. bdg.)
ISBN 0-8368-5323-7 (softcover)

First published in 2003 by
World Almanac® Library
330 West Olive Street, Suite 100
Milwaukee, WI 53212 USA

A Creative Media Applications Production
Design: Alan Barnett, Inc.
Copy editor: Laurie Lieb
Fact checker: Joan Verniero
Photo researcher: Dian Lofton
World Almanac® Library project editor: Tim Paulson
World Almanac® Library editors: Mary Dykstra, Gustav Gedatus, Jacqueline Laks Gorman,
  Lyman Lyons
World Almanac® Library art direction: Tammy Gruenewald
World Almanac® Library graphic designers: Scott M. Krall, Melissa Valuch

Photo credits: pp. 4-5 © Corbis Images; p. 6 (left) © ArtToday; p. 6 (top left) © Corbis Images;
p. 6 (bottom right) © Corbis Images; p. 7 (top) © Photodisc/Getty Images; p. 7 (bottom) © Hulton
Archive; p. 9 © Hulton Archive; p. 10 © CORBIS; p. 11 © Hulton Archive; p. 12 © Hulton
Archive; p. 13 © Hulton Archive; p. 14 © Hulton Archive; p. 15 © Bettmann/CORBIS; p. 17
© Bettmann/CORBIS; p. 18 © Philip Gould/CORBIS; p. 19 © AP Photo/Oxford Eagle, Bruce
Newman; p. 20 (left) Courtesy MS Development Authority; p. 20 (center) © Gary
Braasch/CORBIS; p. 20 (right) © Corbis Images; p. 21 (left) © AP Photo/Oxford Eagle, Bruce
Newman; p. 21 (center) © D. Robert & Lorri Franz/CORBIS; p. 21 (right) Courtesy MS
Development Authority; p. 23 © Corbis Images; p. 26 © Philip Gould/CORBIS; p. 27 © AP
Photo/Mississippi State University, Jim Lytle; p. 29 © Corbis Images; p. 31 (top) © Picture
History; p. 31 (bottom) © Bettmann/CORBIS; p. 32 © David Muench/CORBIS; p. 33 © Danny
Lehman/CORBIS; p. 34 © AP Photo/Rogelio Solis; p. 35 © AP Photo/Rogelio Solis; p. 36 © AP
Photo/Greg Campbell; p. 37 (top) © AP/Wide World Photos; p. 37 (bottom) © AP Photo/Paul
Sakuma; p. 38 © Hulton Archive; p. 39 © AP Photo/Tannen Maury; p. 40 (left) © Hulton
Archive/Getty Images; p. 40 (right) © Hulton Archive/Getty Images; p. 41 (top) © AP/Wide World
Photos; p. 41 (bottom) © Hulton Archive/Getty Images; pp. 42-43 © Hulton Archive/Getty Images;
p. 44 (top) Courtesy MS Development Authority; p. 44 (bottom) Courtesy MS Development
Authority; p. 45 (top) © AP Photo/The Natchez Democrat, Ben Hillyer; p. 45 (bottom) © AP/Wide
World Photos

Printed in the United States of America

2 3 4 5 6 7 8 9 07 06 05 04 03

Mississippi

The Magnolia State

Mississippi is a lushly beautiful state with abundant natural resources. Named after one of the most majestic rivers in the world, the state draws life from the waters of the Mississippi River that flow along its western border. The plants and animals that are nourished by the river have fed the people of this area for thousands of years. The swampy waters of the Delta region are home to catfish, bass, alligators, and bream, while the trees of the state house birds as diverse as doves, hawks, and mockingbirds. Inland forests provide lumber, and cotton flourishes in the hospitable climate.

The arts also thrive in this southern state. Mississippi has produced an amazing number of world-class writers, musicians, and entertainers. Oprah Winfrey, opera star Leontyne Price, Elvis Presley, and playwright Tennessee Williams all hail from Mississippi. The Delta region of this largely rural state gave birth to a type of music called blues that is world famous.

Mississippi played an important role in the growth of the Civil Rights movement in the 1950s and 1960s, when leaders like Martin Luther King Jr. and Medgar Evers fought for the rights of African Americans. As the country watched, Mississippi struggled with and eventually adjusted to a changing world in which all people had equal rights. By the end of the twentieth century, vast strides in racial equality had been made.

Recently, the state has experienced good times with industrial growth and improvement in its educational system. Mississippi has successfully made the transition from farming to industry, improving the standard of living for all Mississippians. At the start of the twenty-first century, Mississippians can look to the future with the expectation that new industries, better schools, and ongoing social reform will lead to an even brighter future.

▶ Map of Mississippi showing the interstate highway system, as well as major cities and waterways.

▼ When cotton bolls mature, they split open, revealing the white fibers. Most of the cotton fields are in western Mississippi.

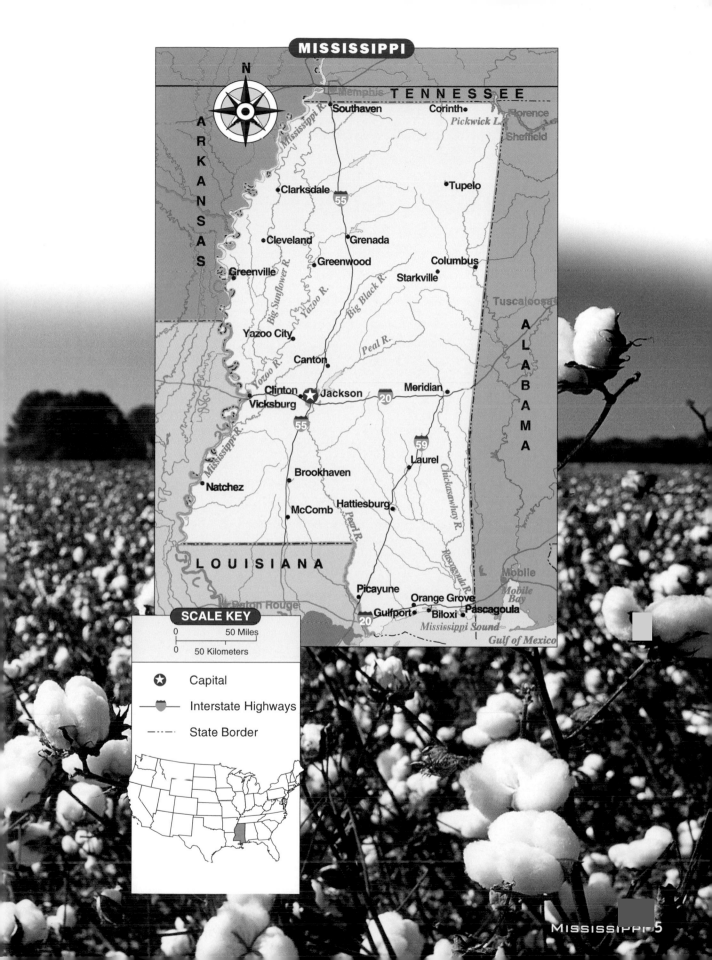

N

ARKANSAS

TENNESSEE

Memphis
Southaven
Corinth
Pickwick L.
Florence
Sheffield

Mississippi R.

Clarksdale
55

Tupelo

Cleveland
Grenada
Columbus

Big Sunflower R.
Greenwood

Greenville
Starkville

Yazoo R.
Big Black R.

Tuscaloosa

Yazoo City

Peal R.

Canton

Clinton
Jackson
Meridian
20

Vicksburg
55

ALABAMA

Yazoo R.

59
Laurel

Mississippi R.

Brookhaven
Chickasawhay R.

Natchez

McComb
Hattiesburg

Pearl R.

LOUISIANA

Pascagoula R.

Mobile

Picayune
Orange Grove
Mobile Bay

Baton Rouge
Gulfport
Biloxi
Pascagoula

20
Mississippi Sound

Gulf of Mexico

Fast Facts

Mississippi (MS), Magnolia State

Entered Union

December 10, 1817 (20th state)

Capital	Population
Jackson	184,256

Total Population (2000)

2,844,656 (31st most populous state)

— *Between 1990 and 2000, the state's population increased 10.5 percent.*

Largest Cities	Population
Jackson	184,256
Gulfport	71,127
Biloxi	50,664
Hattiesburg	44,779
Greenville	41,663

Land Area

46,907 square miles (121,489 square kilometers) (31st largest state)

State Motto

"*Virtute et armis*" Latin for "By valor and arms"

State Song

"Go, Mississippi" *by Houston Davis, date unknown.*

State Bird

Mockingbird — *The mockingbird mimics, or "mocks," the calls of other birds.*

State Fish

Largemouth bass

State Insect

Honeybee

State Marine Mammal

Bottlenose dolphin — *These intelligent sea creatures can be found on the gulf coast of Mississippi.*

State Flower

Magnolia — *This spring-blooming flower has large, waxy petals and a strong fragrance.*

State Tree

Magnolia — *Mississippi is the only state in which the state flower blooms on the state tree.*

State Stone

Petrified wood

State Fossil

Prehistoric whale — *The prehistoric whale was named the state fossil in 1981, after the remains of a zeuglodon were found in the state.*

PLACES TO VISIT

Stanton Hall, *Natchez*
This historic mansion is one of the most visited historic landmarks in Mississippi.

The John C. Stennis Space Center, *Bay St. Louis*
The National Aeronautics and Space Administration (NASA) uses this site to test rockets and other vehicles used in the space program.

Beauvoir, *Biloxi*
The historic seaside estate of Jefferson Davis includes his tomb and the Tomb of the Unknown Confederate Soldier.

For other places and events, see p. 44.

For other places and events, see p. 44.

BIGGEST, BEST, AND MOST

- To make the Tenn-Tom Waterway in northeastern Mississippi, 310 million cubic yards (237 million cubic meters) of earth had to be moved, making it the largest excavation project in history.

- Mississippi has more churches per capita (per person) than any other state.

- Willye B. White is the only female athlete to compete in five consecutive Olympic summer games. She competed in track and field events beginning in 1956.

STATE FIRSTS

- **1818** The first U. S. women's college, Elizabeth Female Academy, was chartered in the town of Washington.

- **1863** The first Memorial Day observance was held at the Friendship Cemetery in Columbus to honor Civil War soldiers.

- **1870** Reverend Hiram R. Revels became the first African American elected U.S. Senator.

- **1949** William Grant Still became the first African-American composer to have an opera performed by a major opera company.

The Flexible Flyer — Built in Mississippi

In the 1860s, Samuel Leeds Allen, a well-to-do Quaker from Philadelphia, founded a company that manufactured farm equipment. He soon realized that his firm had very little business during the cold winter months. In the 1880s as a lark, Allen decided to build a sled with a unique design: the rider steered the sled with a crossbar that controlled two steel runners. The new sled was sold as a "flexible flyer," a name that caught on with the public. The sleds became the most popular sled in the country. Flexible Flyers are now made in West Point, Mississippi.

Stickball, a Choctaw Sport

The oldest organized game in this country is stickball, played by the Choctaw tribe of Mississippi. The game had already been played for centuries when the first European settlers arrived in what is now Mississippi. Players were required to play barefoot. The most distinguished stickball player of the Choctaw was Tullock-Chish-ko, or "he who drinks the juice of the stone." The game, and a variation called Lacrosse, is still played across the United States.

Natural Beauty and Social Upheaval

> If we had been allowed to participate in the vital processes of America's national growth ... We black folk say that America would have been stronger and greater.
>
> — *Author Richard Wright,* Twelve Million Black Voices, *1941*

Approximately 10,000 years ago, the first settlers arrived in what is now known as Mississippi. These early people settled in the area and multiplied. By the sixteenth century, several Native American tribes flourished. Three tribes, the Choctaw, the Natchez, and the Chickasaw, controlled most of the land. Each of the three had distinct practices that helped them prosper. The Natchez were a highly organized society that developed strict laws. The powerful Choctaw built fortified villages that served to protect them from enemies. The warlike Chickasaw controlled large tracts of land by setting up their villages in lines that stretched for miles.

European Exploration and Settlement

The first Europeans to enter the area were from Spain. Hernando de Soto was serving as governor of Cuba when he heard tales of a land with many gold mines. In 1539, he set off with six hundred men on a journey in search of gold through what is now Florida, Georgia, South Carolina, Alabama, Mississippi, and Arkansas. De Soto's trek wasn't easy. In the Pontotoc Battle of 1541, the Chickasaw killed many of his men.

De Soto spent three years searching for gold, without success. He died and was buried in the Mississippi River in 1542. European explorers returned in 1673, when a Jesuit minister, Father Jacques Marquette, and a fur trapper, Louis Jolliet, explored the region. They traveled by boat, starting at the Great Lakes, and headed south to the point where the Mississippi River meets the Arkansas River. After exploring the area, they returned to Canada.

Native Americans of Mississippi
Chickasaw
Choctaw
Natchez
Pascagoula
Tunica
Westo
Yazoo

DID YOU KNOW?

The Natchez tribe used a rigid class structure. Three groups of nobility ruled the tribe. The most powerful group was known as the Suns. Ordinary tribespeople were called Stinkards. The chief of the Natchez was so revered that his feet were never allowed to touch the ground.

European Rule

In 1682, René-Robert Cavelier, Sieur de la Salle, having fought and won large parcels of land from the Natchez tribe, claimed for France all of the land drained by the Mississippi River. He called this region Louisiana, in honor of the king of France, Louis XIV. The first capital of this huge French colony of North America, Fort Maurepas, was established near the present-day town of Ocean Springs in 1699. Within twenty years, a second French settlement was established about 160 miles (260 km) away at Fort Rosalie, the site of present-day Natchez. On this fertile land, in soil enriched by the river, colonists grew cotton, rice, tobacco, and indigo, which was used to dye fabric blue.

The French colonists had two enemies in the early eighteenth century. The Natchez were angry that the French had taken their land, and British troops were fighting to take control of North America. Eventually, these two groups formed an alliance to take the land from the French. As part of this effort, two hundred French settlers were killed at Fort Rosalie in 1729. This attack led to widespread retaliation by the French, in which most of the Natchez were killed or enslaved. The warlike Chickasaw also sided with the British and defeated the French at the Battle of Ackia in 1736.

▼ **Father Marquette and Louis Jolliet, along with five other explorers, headed south on the Mississippi River.**

France's control over the area ended with the French and Indian War (1754–1763). Great Britain won the war and acquired the land east of the Mississippi River, all of which had belonged to the French.

Becoming a Part of the United States

By the end of the eighteenth century, the new United States government had won the land east of the Mississippi River from the British in the Revolutionary War (1775–1783). In 1798, the U.S. Congress named Natchez as the capital of the territory of Mississippi, and President John Adams appointed the territory's first governor, Winthrop Sargent. In 1803, the United States purchased the Louisiana Territory, a huge tract of land west of the Mississippi River, from France. This opened the Mississippi River to U.S. commerce, which in turn led to clashes with the Spanish government, which ruled the Gulf Coast from New Orleans to Florida. American settlers in Florida began fighting the Spanish for more land, taking control of everything from the Mississippi River east to the Perdido River. By 1812, the Mississippi Territory included all of the land that now makes up the states of Mississippi and Alabama.

DID YOU KNOW?

The Mississippi Territory's borders changed significantly between 1798 and 1817. At one time, the territory was almost twice as large as the current state.

▼ In this nineteenth century drawing, a sidewheel steamboat nears a dock at a plantation along the Mississippi River. The steamboat was a primary source of transporting both goods and people during this time.

Statehood

In 1817, the U.S. Congress divided the Mississippi Territory into the state of Mississippi and the Alabama Territory, and on December 10, 1817, Mississippi entered the union as the twentieth state. Based on the census of 1817 and historians' estimates, Mississippi's population was made up of 25,000 whites, 23,000 black slaves, and 35,000 Native Americans, mostly Choctaw and Chickasaw. Native Americans controlled two-thirds of the land in the state. As migrants from the east crowded the area, the state legislature and the courts pressured the Choctaw and Chickasaw to give up their land. By 1832, both tribes had agreed to move to the Indian Territory in what is now Oklahoma. The Chickasaw alone ceded more than 6 million acres (2.4 million hectares). This huge piece of available land lured even more settlers to Mississippi, drawn by the fertile soil and favorable growing conditions that would fuel the state's economy for years to come. By 1822, when the state capital was moved to Jackson, Mississippi was one of the wealthiest states in the Union.

The Road to the Civil War

The rich soil meant that Mississippi was a land of opportunity for anyone willing to farm. By 1860, approximately thirty thousand Mississippians used slave labor on their farms. This angered many people from the northern states who considered slavery immoral, as well as unfair to the businesses in states that did not permit slavery. By the middle of the nineteenth century, slavery was the most important political issue in Congress, with the South in favor and the North opposed. This issue caused such anger among Southerners that they began to consider the idea of secession, or breaking away from the United States. At first, few Mississippians were in favor of this drastic measure, but by the 1850s, as the federal government pushed the South to abolish slavery, the idea became more popular.

Pierre Le Moyne

Pierre Le Moyne, Sieur d'Iberville, was the son of a man who came to the New World as a servant and quickly made his fortune as a fur trader. Le Moyne fought with the French against the English in North America and led his men to several important victories. He went to France in 1697, and in 1698, he led an expedition to explore what is now Louisiana, establishing the first permanent French settlement in 1699 at what is now Ocean Springs, Mississippi.

A fearless and successful soldier and explorer, Le Moyne was described by a contemporary, Dr. John Clarence Webster, as "spread[ing] terror . . . all along the Atlantic seaboard." Le Moyne died in Havana in 1706.

Secession and the Civil War

When Abraham Lincoln was elected president in 1860, it became clear that he would act swiftly to free the slaves. With its economy at stake, the South remained firm in its conviction that slavery must not be abolished, and states began to secede from the Union. On January 19, 1861, Mississippi became the second state to secede. By the time the Civil War started, a total of eleven states had joined the Confederate States of America, with Jefferson Davis as their president.

Fighting broke out on April 12, 1861, when Confederate soldiers fired on Fort Sumter in South Carolina. In April 1862, the Battle of Shiloh, fought along the Mississippi-Tennessee border, ended in a defeat for the Confederacy. The most famous conflict fought in Mississippi was the Battle of Vicksburg in 1863. The Union blocked the Mississippi River and its harbors so that supplies could not make their way to the Confederate soldiers and civilians in Vicksburg who needed them. For six weeks, the Union army bombarded the city without stopping. The people of Vicksburg eventually ran out of food and drinking water.

▼ The Battle of Vicksburg was one of the most important Civil War battles. The victory gave the Union Army control of the Mississippi River.

Finally, on July 4, 1863, Confederate general John C. Pemberton surrendered the city, after 10,000 Union soldiers and 30,000 Confederate soldiers were killed or wounded in the siege. The war ended on April 9, 1865 when Confederate general Robert E. Lee surrendered to Union general Ulysses S. Grant at Appomattox Courthouse, Virginia.

Reconstruction

During the years from 1865 to 1877, known as the period of Reconstruction, a series of conflicts arose. The federal government was intent on establishing control over the wayward Southern states, a situation that angered many southerners. The new state government of Mississippi, elected in October 1865, was made up primarily of former Confederates. This government quickly enacted "the Black Codes," legislation that made it virtually impossible for African Americans to live as free people. They were denied the right to vote and required to obey strict rules on how and when they could change jobs — rules that made it easier for employers to treat them unfairly. African Americans were unable to rent land in urban areas, serve on juries, or hold public office.

When Mississippi refused to accept the Fourteenth Amendment, which granted citizenship to former slaves, Congress placed the state under military rule. Mississippi would not be allowed to be part of the Union until it adopted a new state constitution that was acceptable to the federal government. In May 1868, Mississippi finally adopted the new constitution, which guaranteed African Americans the right to vote and outlawed racial discrimination. On February 23, 1870, Mississippi was readmitted to the Union.

Hiram R. Revels, U.S. Senator

Born in 1822, Revels attended schools in Fayetteville and Knox College in Galesburg, Illinois. He organized two regiments of African Americans during the Civil War and later started a school for freedmen in St. Louis, Missouri. In 1870, he became the first African American to be elected to the U.S. Senate. After leaving the Senate, he worked as an educator. Revels died in 1901 in Aberdeen, Mississippi.

Jim Crow and Hard Times

By 1875, ex-Confederates had once again gained political power in the state. New "Jim Crow" state laws denied African Americans their basic rights and enforced segregation policies. By using the threat of physical violence, the Ku Klux Klan promoted white supremacy and prevented African Americans from voting. Then in 1890, a new state constitution was adopted that virtually stripped African Americans of their civil rights. The new laws made it all but impossible for any African American to vote. At the same time, white landowners charged the freed slaves such high rent for the use of the land that it kept the former slaves in debt. This constitution and the harsh financial situation created a difficult way of life for African Americans in Mississippi that lasted for more than seventy years.

Entering the Twentieth Century

During the early years of the twentieth century, the people of Mississippi struggled financially. Segregation laws, inadequate schools, and a poor standard of living — most rural residents of Mississippi did not have electricity at this time — made life in many areas of the state difficult. As a result of these conditions, thousands of African-American Mississippians left their homes to work in Northern factories that produced ammunition, ships, and other goods needed during World War I.

When the United States entered World War II (1941–1945), Mississippi finally began to experience economic growth. Close to 250,000 men and women enlisted in the armed forces, ensuring steady paychecks for their families at home. At the same time, shipyards, military bases, and the businesses that serve the military were established throughout the state. Local farmers also benefited from this economic boom, as military bases bought local produce, meat, and dairy products to feed the soldiers.

The Civil Rights Era and Beyond

In 1954, when the U.S. Supreme Court decided that segregation in public schools was illegal, many Southern states refused to integrate not only their schools, but also other public places such as theaters and bus stations. At this time, the Civil Rights Movement, which sought equal rights for all people, became a powerful force throughout the United States. Civil rights leaders like Martin Luther

DID YOU KNOW?

The siege of Vicksburg was a smart military move, for it affected both the soldiers and civilians. By the end of the battle, people in Vicksburg had run out of food and drinking water.

King Jr. visited Mississippi to protest conditions for African Americans, and U.S. officials acted to protect their rights. In 1962, President John F. Kennedy sent federal troops to the campus of the University of Mississippi to force the administration to allow an African-American student to enroll. Soldiers remained on campus for over a year to keep order after a demonstration in which two people died and over three hundred were injured. In 1965, President Lyndon B. Johnson signed the Voting Rights Act, which forced all Southern states to allow African Americans to vote. In 1969, a federal court ordered Mississippi to desegregate its schools.

During these years of important social change, life for Mississippians improved in other ways as well. The economic improvements that occurred during World War II continued as the per capita (per person) income rose steadily, industries built factories in the area, and unemployment dropped.

Charles Evers

Charles Evers was the first African-American mayor in Mississippi since Reconstruction. After his brother, Medgar Evers, was assassinated in 1963, Charles took over his job as field secretary of the Mississippi chapter of the National Association for the Advancement of Colored People, a civil rights organization founded in 1909.

Charles Evers served as mayor of Fayette from 1969 to 1981 and again from 1985 to 1989.

Mississippi Rising

> I've been asked all over America ... why Mississippi is so distinctive. You know, we have our failings, but we're coming along all right.
>
> — *Author Willie Morris,* Conversations with Willie Morris, *2000*

From 1990 to 2000, Mississippi's population grew by more than 10 percent. In the year 2000, the total population was 2,844,656. Fifty-one percent of Mississippians live in rural areas as compared to forty-nine percent living in urban areas. The percentage of people living in urban areas is much lower than in other states. Since 1940, however, the number of people living in the cities has been steadily growing as people leave farming to work in the many thriving urban industries. Urban residents are divided among cities such as Jackson, with 184,256 residents, Gulfport (71,127), and Biloxi (50,644). Jackson is the principal manufacturing and commercial center in the state; Gulfport is a major shipping center as well as a resort town; and Biloxi has a thriving fishing and food-processing industry.

Age distribution in Mississippi
(2000 Census)

0–4	204,364
5–19	668,850
20–24	212,947
25–44	807,170
45–64	607,804
65 & over	343,523

Across One Hundred Years

Mississippi's three largest foreign-born groups for 1890 and 1990

	1890	1990
Germany	2,284	
Ireland	1,865	
England	884	
Vietnam		2,284
Germany		1,807
United Kingdom		1,694

Total state population: 1,289,600
Total foreign-born: 7,952 (0.6%)

Total state population: 2,573,216
Total foreign-born: 20,383 (0.8%)

Patterns of Immigration

The total number of people who immigrated to Mississippi in 1998 was 701. Of that number, the largest immigrant groups were from India (13.4%), China (9.8%), and the Philippines (9.1%).

Ethnicities

The first European settlers in Mississippi were French, followed by the British. After the French left the area, the British flourished. That early influence is evident in the ethnic backgrounds of most Mississippians. The majority are Caucasians of British, Irish, and Northern European descent. Chinese immigrants came to Mississippi in the 1870s and established themselves as merchants. This small community still exists in present-day Mississippi. In the years after 1940, a steady stream of African Americans left the state in search of better jobs in the Northeast, as factories opened that offered opportunity for work and the hope of a better environment for African Americans. A small group of Choctaw live in the east-central part of the state.

▲ Early settlers of European ancestry established plantations in Mississippi and often brought slaves from Africa to work in the fields.

Religion

The early years of settlement resulted in several shifts in religious affiliation in Mississippi. The first settlers were Roman Catholic, so Catholicism became the official religion of the colony. When the British took control of the area, the Church of England became the official religion. Today, the majority of Mississippians are Protestant, with Baptists

DID YOU KNOW?

Most African-American Mississippians live in the Delta, the low-lying land near the Mississippi River. African Americans make up 60 percent of the population in some counties.

Heritage and Background, Mississippi — Year 2000

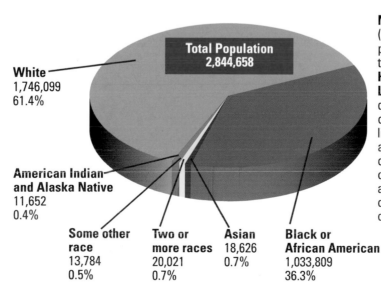

▶ Here is a look at the racial backgrounds of Mississippians today. Mississippi ranks first among U.S. states with regard to African Americans as a percentage of the population.

Total Population 2,844,658

White 1,746,099 61.4%

American Indian and Alaska Native 11,652 0.4%

Some other race 13,784 0.5%

Two or more races 20,021 0.7%

Asian 18,626 0.7%

Black or African American 1,033,809 36.3%

Note: 1.4% (39,589) of the population identify themselves as **Hispanic** or **Latino,** a cultural designation that crosses racial lines. Hispanics and Latinos are counted in this category as well as the racial category of their choice.

and Methodists making up the largest segments. Several of Mississippi's cities have sizeable Jewish communities. There are synagogues in Meridian, Clarksdale, and Jackson.

Education

English settlers founded the first schools in Mississippi in the eighteenth century. Although the first free public school, Franklin Academy, opened in 1821 in Columbus, there was no statewide public school system until the 1840s. In 1862, the first public school for African Americans was founded, followed in 1870 by a statewide public school system designed to provide education for all students. It was not until 1918 that state legislation was passed requiring all school-age children to attend school.

Educational Levels of Mississippi Workers (age 25 and over)	
Less than 9th grade.	169,178
9th to 12th grade, no diploma.	307,852
High school graduate, including equivalency	516,091
Some college, no degree or associate degree	467,305
Bachelor's degree.	194,325
Graduate or professional degree	102,766

▼ The skyline of Jackson, Mississippi's capital and largest city.

Public education in Mississippi underwent a very difficult period in the 1950s and 1960s as white Mississippians struggled to prevent racial integration. In 1954, the U.S. Supreme Court declared racial segregation in public schools to be unconstitutional, a decision that angered many white Mississippians. To help prevent African Americans from attending white schools, the state abolished the law requiring school attendance. In 1962, to ensure that African Americans would have a fair chance in Mississippi's schools, the federal government stepped in and forced the University of Mississippi to admit an African-American student, James Meredith. In 1964, fifty-seven African-American elementary students were admitted to what had been all-white public schools. Even with this progress, it was not until 1986 that school attendance was made mandatory again. Today, ten percent of Mississippi's children attend private schools.

The state's first college was founded in 1802 as Jefferson College in Natchez. Mississippi now has twenty-six public and sixteen private institutions of higher education. The oldest still in operation is Mississippi College in Clinton. Originally called Hampstead Academy, it was founded in 1826. Alcorn State University, founded in 1871, was the nation's first state-supported institution for the higher education of African Americans. Today it has approximately three thousand students and offers both bachelor's and master's degrees. Alcorn State has intercollegiate teams for men in several sports, among them baseball, basketball, and football. It has teams for women in basketball, tennis, track and field, volleyball, and other sports. The University of Mississippi, or "Ole Miss," was founded in 1848. In its first year, eighty students enrolled for classes. By 2002, the university had 14,500 students, of whom 13 percent were African American.

▲ The University of Mississippi is often called by its nickname "Ole Miss."

Mississippi State University

Mississippi State University was founded in 1878 as the Agricultural and Mechanical College of the State of Mississippi. During the years since its founding, the school has expanded to include degrees in science, engineering, and the humanities.

Plains and Coastline

> . . . how curiously the strange and the familiar
> were mixed together . . .
> — *Author Mark Twain,* Life on the Mississippi, *1863*

Mississippi, home to the third-largest river in the world, is a place of awesome natural beauty and resources. It is the thirty-first largest state in the United States in land area, with an area of 46,907 square miles (121,489 sq km). At its widest point, Mississippi measures 180 miles (290 kilometers) east to west. Its length, from its border with Tennessee to the Gulf of Mexico, measures 340 miles (547 km). Mississippi shares borders with Tennessee, Alabama, Arkansas, and Louisiana. The western border runs along the Mississippi River itself, and as a result, it shifted frequently in the past as the river changed its course. Mississippi can be divided into two distinct regions, the Delta, or Mississippi Alluvial Plain, and the East Gulf Coastal Plain.

THE DELTA

Located in the western part of the state, the Delta is the result of thousands of years of flooding in the area. Whenever the Mississippi River rose, its waters overflowed its banks, leaving tons of nutrient-rich alluvial soil spread

Highest Point
Woodall Mountain
806 feet (246 meters)
above sea level

▼ *From left to right*:
**Ross Barnett
Reservoir; a
Mississippi alligator;
black-eyed Susans;
a fisherman at Sardis
Lake; a white-tailed
deer; cypress swamp.**

over thousands of square miles. The products of this agricultural soil have fueled Mississippi's economy since the time of its earliest settlers. The southernmost part of the Delta, known as the river lowlands, measures less than 1 mile (1.6 km) across near Natchez. Moving north past Vicksburg, the Delta widens to about 65 miles (105 km) near Greenville. This part of the Delta originally was covered with swamps, but settlers drained much of it to use as farmland in the nineteenth century.

The East Gulf Coastal Plain

All of the land east of the Delta is known as the East Gulf Coastal Plain. The highest point in this region (and in the entire state) is Woodall Mountain in the Northeastern Hills. The elevation decreases as one moves south to the gulf coast. The coast, known for its sandy beaches and warm water, is protected from the open ocean by a series of offshore islands. The shoreline, running in and out of numerous bays and coves, measures 359 miles (578 km). This area has been popular with tourists for much of the twentieth century.

The Mississippi River

The Mississippi River has shaped the lives of those who have lived near it for thousands of years. Flowing through channels left by glaciers that melted over ten thousand years ago, the river is the largest drainage system in North America, averaging 593,000 cubic feet (16,800 cubic meters) per second of water at its mouth. Its average width in Mississippi ranges from 3,000 to 5,000 feet (914 to 1,524 meters). The river is home to much animal life, from catfish and clams to loons and armadillos. Unfortunately for the environment, the river also serves to process sewage and industrial pollutants. These waste products are dumped

Average January temperature
Jackson: 45°F (7.2°C)
Vicksburg: 47°F (8.3°C)

Average July temperature
Jackson: 81°F (27.2°C)
Vicksburg: 82°F (27.8°C)

Average yearly rainfall
Jackson:
 56 inches (142 cm)
Vicksburg:
 58 inches (147 cm)

DID YOU KNOW?

Mississippi has no large natural lakes. All of the lakes listed below were created artificially. The Ross Barnett Reservoir was formed by building an earth-filled dam. It is overseen by a state agency.

Largest Lakes

Ross Barnett Reservoir
33,000 acres (13,360 ha)

Sardis Lake
32,500 acres (13,200 ha)

Arkabutla Lake
11,200 acres (4,500 ha)

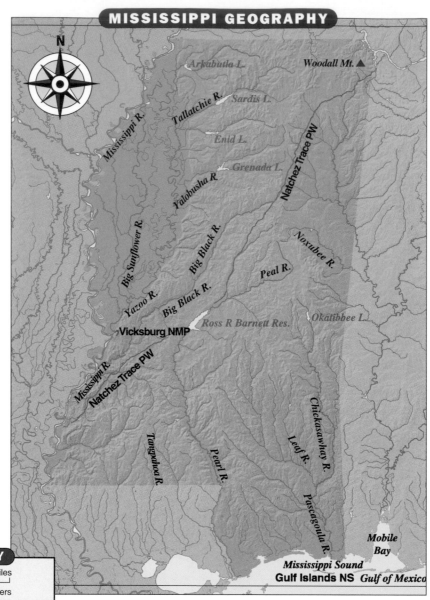

Map labels:

Arkabutla L.
Woodall Mt. ▲
Tallatchie R.
Sardis L.
Mississippi R.
Enid L.
Natchez Trace PW
Grenada L.
Yalobusha R.
Big Sunflower R.
Big Black R.
Noxubee R.
Peal R.
Yazoo R.
Big Black R.
Big Black R.
Okatibbee L.
Vicksburg NMP
Ross R Barnett Res.
Mississippi R.
Natchez Trace PW
Chickasawhay R.
Leaf R.
Tangipahoa R.
Pearl R.
Pascagoula R.
Mobile Bay
Mississippi Sound
Gulf Islands NS
Gulf of Mexico

SCALE/KEY

| 0 | 50 Miles |
| 0 | 50 Kilometers |

NMP	National Military Park
NS	National Seashore
PW	Parkway
▲	Highest Point
▓	Mountains

directly into the river and allowed to flow out to sea. State organizations and private groups are working to clean up this amazing natural resource.

Plants and Animals

Settlers in the eighteenth and nineteenth centuries cleared large portions of the state's land, which was once covered almost entirely with forests. Recently, efforts have been made to replant abandoned farmland. Tree species in Mississippi include oak, tulip, and sycamore trees in the Northeastern Hills and swamp oaks, sweet gums, and eastern cottonwoods in the Delta. The state flower, the magnolia, grows on the tree of the same name throughout the state. Its waxy white or pink flowers bloom in the spring. Other common flowering trees of the region include azaleas, dogwoods, and rhododendrons.

The wet pine savannas of Mississippi are home to an interesting group of carnivorous plants. The extremely acidic soil in this area is lacking in nutrients, and so these plants have adapted by developing, over time, the ability to capture and eat insects. There are ten species of carnivorous plants in Mississippi, among them the bladderwort and the pitcher plant.

Although big-game animals such as the bison and the cougar that lived in the area long ago have disappeared, most species of wildlife have continued to flourish. The largest mammal, the white-tailed deer, is relatively common in the forests, along with foxes, armadillos, and raccoons. The swampy Delta is home to alligators, pelicans, and the state bird, the mockingbird. Snakes are plentiful, including the poisonous coral snake, copperhead, and rattlesnake, and the nonpoisonous garter snake. The state is also home to many species of bird, including the brown-headed nuthatch and the red-cockaded woodpecker.

Major Rivers

Mississippi River
2,340 miles (3,765 km)

Big Black River
330 miles (531 km)

Yazoo River
169 miles (272 km)

▼ The mighty Mississippi River is spanned by twin bridges at Natchez.

Riches from the River

> The only way the magic works is by hard work.
> But the hard work can be fun.
>
> — *Jim Henson, creator of the Muppets*

When European settlers first arrived in Mississippi, they were amazed at the rich soil and long growing season. These conditions made agriculture a profitable basis for the state's economy until changes brought about by the Civil War made it more difficult for farmers to make a living. As a result, until the start of World War II, Mississippi struggled economically. When manufacturers began to open factories in the 1940s, the standard of living improved and this trend has continued to the present. Today, the once-important agricultural industry provides work for very few Mississippians, and the number of farms has decreased dramatically. Now, the service industry, wholesale and retail trade, and manufacturing shape the economy of the state. With a work force of nearly 1.3 million people, unemployment in 2000 was 5.7 percent. At the same time, the poverty rate fell, from 25.2 percent in 1989 to 14.5 percent in 2000.

From Sofas to Salami

Manufacturing is a key part of the state's renewed economy. Starting in 1936, when Governor Hugh White started a program called Balance Agriculture With Industry, manufacturers in the state have steadily increased both in number and diversity. Mississippi is the nation's largest producer of upholstered furniture, with factory sales estimated at $1.2 billion dollars. Shipbuilding and auto-parts factories employ large numbers of Mississippians. Ingall's Shipyard in Pascagoula employs over ten thousand workers. Food products such as packaged meats and

Top Employers
(of workers age sixteen and over)

Services	38.4%
Manufacturing	18.3%
Wholesale and retail trade	15.2%
Construction	7.6%
Transportation, communications, and public utilities	7.2%
Federal, state, and local government (including military)	5.1%
Finance, insurance, and real estate	4.8%
Agriculture, forestry, fisheries, and mining	3.4%

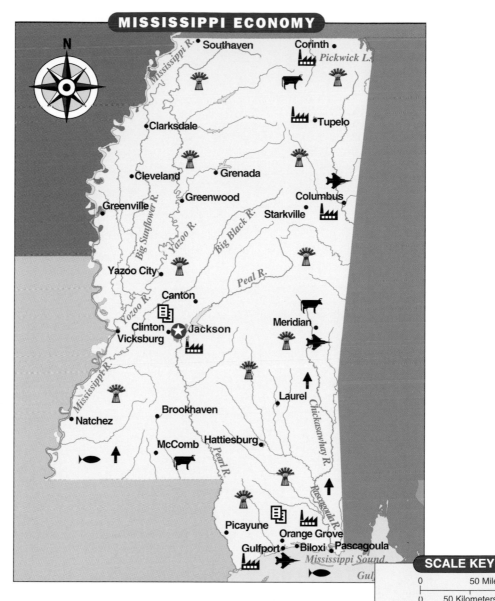

MISSISSIPPI ECONOMY

N

Southaven
Corinth
Pickwick L.

Clarksdale

Tupelo

Cleveland
Grenada

Greenwood

Columbus

Greenville

Starkville

Yazoo City

Canton

Meridian

Clinton · Jackson
Vicksburg

Laurel

Natchez
Brookhaven

McComb
Hattiesburg

Picayune

Orange Grove
Gulfport · Biloxi · Pascagoula
Mississippi Sound
Gul

Mississippi R.
Big Sunflower R.
Yazoo R.
Big Black R.
Peal R.
Yazoo R.
Mississippi R.
Pearl R.
Chickasawhay R.
R......la R.

SCALE KEY

| 0 | 50 Miles |
| 0 | 50 Kilometers |

🐄 Cattle/Dairy

🌾 Farming

🐟 Fishing

↑ Forestry

🏭 Manufacturing

✈ Military

📇 Services

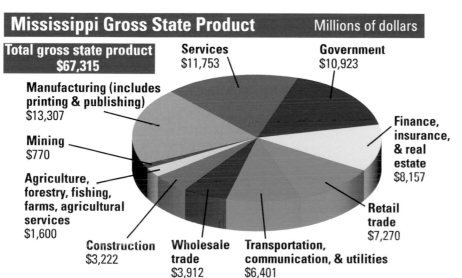

Mississippi Gross State Product   Millions of dollars

Total gross state product $67,315

Services $11,753

Government $10,923

Manufacturing (includes printing & publishing) $13,307

Finance, insurance, & real estate $8,157

Mining $770

Agriculture, forestry, fishing, farms, agricultural services $1,600

Retail trade $7,270

Construction $3,222

Wholesale trade $3,912

Transportation, communication, & utilities $6,401

prepared seafood also contribute to the state's economy. Millions of acres of land that were cleared for farming in the nineteenth century have been replanted with trees and are being managed as pine plantations. Pine trees, as well as hardwood trees such as oak and hickory in the northern part of the state, are cut and processed for lumber.

▲ The Mississippi River continues to be a rich source of food — and income — for the state.

Food from the Earth, Food from the Sea

Although farming is no longer the main industry of the state, Mississippi still produces a wide range of crops and animal products. Crops provided 30 percent of the farm income in the year 2000. Mississippi is the nation's fourth-largest producer of cotton, after Texas, California, and Georgia. Cotton generates more income for the state than any other crop, with soybeans second. Cattle, poultry, and dairy products are major sources of income in the southern and eastern parts of the state. "Broilers," or five-to-twelve-week-old chickens, are the leading source of livestock income. Mississippi has over 100,000 acres (40,500 ha) of catfish ponds and produces the most farm-raised catfish of any state in the country. Mississippi catfish growers generated $271 million in 2001.

HELPING OTHERS, HELPING THEMSELVES

The service industry is one of the top employers in the state. Service industries include restaurants, hotels, airlines, law firms, grocery stores, private hospitals, and

A Farm for Fish?

If you think farms only exist on land, think again. Mississippi has many farms that produce one "crop" — catfish! In a catfish farm, the fish are raised in environments that reproduce the best possible natural conditions: the right water temperature, adequate food, and protection from predators. Using this method, Mississippi produces catfish that are shipped all over the world. Catfish are not the only type of fish raised this way. Other fish and shellfish routinely farmed in other states include salmon, trout, mussels, and clams.

doctors' offices. More than one-third of all Mississippians are employed in this industry. Mississippi has become a popular tourist destination, with people from all over the country traveling to the Gulf Coast and the Delta. In order to accommodate these visitors, hotels, shops, restaurants, and airlines have flourished. Government agencies are another important part of the economic life of Mississippi. Educational facilities, public hospitals, and the military all provide jobs and income to the people of the state.

▲ Most Mississippi catfish farms are located in the Delta region. Catfish farming is a form of aquaculture, the science and business of growing fish and other freshwater and marine animals for food.

Highway to Prosperity

When Mississippi lawmakers voted to begin the Four-Lane Highway Program in 1987, their decision led to an additional $4.1 billion in economic activity in the state. The new highways, which will cover 1,700 miles (2,735 km) when finished, have cost over $2 billion so far, but have allowed people to travel easily throughout the state. According to one estimate, the safer roads led to a reduction in traffic deaths, with eighty-six lives saved in 1998. The highways have helped Mississippi's manufacturers to ship their goods north to their customers. The lumber, processed food, and furniture industries' increased revenue is due, in part, to this new highway. It has led to new business opportunities and has helped add many jobs throughout the state, including highway repair positions. Mississippi expects to spend $80 million every year to keep the new highways in good shape.

Made in Mississippi

Leading farm products and crops
Broilers (chickens)
Cotton
Soybeans
Lumber
Cattle
Corn

Other products
Processed foods
Chemicals (drugs and fertilizers)
Plastics
Furniture

Major Airports		
Airport	Location	Passengers per year (2000)
Jackson International	Jackson	1,360,280

Of the People, By the People

> We failed, but in the good providence of God apparent failure often proves a blessing.
> — *Robert E. Lee, Confederate General*

The constitution of 1890 is the fourth in Mississippi's history, with the first three adopted in 1817, 1832, and 1869. The 1890 constitution did not effectively serve the entire population of the state, however, until the Voting Rights Act of 1965 gave all Mississippians, including African Americans, the right to vote. And so — 158 years after the first adopted constitution — all people in Mississippi finally had equal rights.

To make a change in the constitution, a two-thirds majority of the state legislature must request it. Next, to ensure that Mississippi's citizens can play an active role in their government, the amendment is put to a vote in a general election. Another way to amend the constitution is if a majority of the members of each house of the state legislature calls for a constitutional convention.

Mississippi's state government mirrors the structure of the federal government in Washington, D.C. The executive branch, the legislative branch, and the judicial branch have their own responsibilities and powers. Combined, the three branches keep a balance of power — no branch is more powerful than another.

The Executive Branch

The governor is the chief executive official of the state and handles the state's business and enforces its laws. Mississippi's governors serve a four-year term, with a maximum of two consecutive terms. Independently or with the approval of the senate, the governor appoints other officials to run the agencies and commissions that help govern the state. The governor can also approve or veto laws passed by the legislature. Voters elect the governor,

State Constitution

"**A**ll political power is vested in, and derived from, the people; all government of right originates with the people, is founded upon their will only, and is instituted for the good of the whole."

—*1890 Constitution of Mississippi, adopted November 1, 1890*

Elected Posts in the Executive Branch		
Office	Length of Term	Term Limits
Governor	4 years	2 consecutive terms
Lieutenant Governor	4 years	2 consecutive terms
Secretary of State	4 years	none
Commissioner of Insurance	4 years	none
Attorney General	4 years	none
Auditor	4 years	none
Commissioner of Agriculture	4 years	none

the lieutenant governor, the secretary of state, and the attorney general, and several other executive positions that monitor everything from elections to law enforcement.

The Legislative Branch

As the U.S. Congress creates the laws for the country, the legislative branch makes the laws for Mississippi. The state legislature has two separate chambers, the senate and the house of representatives. The senate has 52 members and the house has 122 members that each serve four-year terms. The elections are set up so that every two years half of the members are eligible for re-election. The legislature begins its sessions on the Tuesday after the first Monday in January. Regular sessions are held annually, with a limit of 125 days in the first year of a new governor's term and in all even-numbered years. Sessions in odd-numbered years are limited to ninety days.

▼ Built in 1903, the state capitol building in Jackson rests on the site of an old penitentiary.

The legislature proposes and passes new laws, proposes amendments to the state constitution, and is able to override the governor's veto of a new law. A two-thirds majority of both houses is necessary to override any veto.

The Mississippi Senate and House meet in the Mississippi State Capitol, which was built in 1903 and is modeled after the nation's Capitol in Washington, D.C. In contrast to most statehouses, the Mississippi State Capitol was designed with the podium at the back of the room, so that when people enter, they must turn around to face the speaker. Like the United States Capitol building, the Mississippi State Capitol building has a large dome, on top of which stands an eagle with a 15-foot (4.6 m) wingspan.

The Judicial Branch

The executive branch and the legislative branch create and enforce the laws of the state, but the judicial branch interprets and applies the laws. The highest court in Mississippi is the state supreme court, to which voters elect nine justices that serve eight-year terms. The chief justice of the supreme court is the judge who has served the longest. Below the supreme court are the chancery courts and the circuit courts. These are the main trial courts of the state. Chancery courts hear civil (noncriminal) cases, while circuit courts hear both civil and criminal cases. Combined, these two courts have seventy-nine judges. The remaining courts are the county, municipal, justice, and family courts. Judges in the circuit, chancery, and lower courts serve terms of four years.

Local Government

The state of Mississippi is divided into eighty-two counties. Each county is governed by a board of five supervisors, elected for four-year terms. In addition to the board of supervisors, each county has a variety of other officials, including sheriff, superintendent of education, and attorney, also elected for four-year terms. The oldest county in

State Legislature			
House	Number of Members	Length of Term	Term Limits
Senate	52 senators	4 years	No limit
House of Representatives	122 representatives	4 years	No limit

Mississippi is Adams County, one of the two counties created by Governor Winthrop Sargent's proclamation of April 2, 1799. Adams County was one of the two original counties of the Natchez District. It was named for John Adams, who at that time was president of the United States. Of the approximately 500 cities and towns throughout Mississippi, 294 have an organized city government with an elected mayor and alderman.

National Representation

Like all states, Mississippi elects two senators to the U.S. Senate. Mississippi also elects five members to the U.S. House of Representatives. Members of the House serve two-year terms, while senators serve six-year terms.

Mississippi Politics

Mississippi was a strongly Democratic state from its acceptance into the union until late in the twentieth century. Mississippi cast its electoral votes for the Democratic candidate for president in every election from 1876 through 1944. In the years since, Mississippi cast its votes for third-party presidential candidates who favored segregation in the elections of 1948, 1960, and 1968. In most elections since 1968, Mississippi has cast its votes for the Republican candidate.

▼ In this 1946 photograph, African Americans vote in the Mississippi Democratic Party primary for the first time since adoption of the State Constitution in 1890. More than one thousand African Americans voted in the former home of Senator Bilbo in Jackson.

Adelbert Ames

Born in 1835 in Maine, Adelbert Ames served in the Union Army during the Civil War. After serving as General George G. Meade's assistant in the Battle of Chancellorville, Ames commanded a division at the Battle of Gettysburg. A dedicated soldier, Ames eventually reached the rank of Major General. When the Civil War ended, Ames entered politics. He served as Mississippi's provisional governor, as its U.S. Senator, and finally as its elected governor. Ames appointed Hiram Revels to the Natchez Board of Alderman, thereby starting the African American on his political career. Ames did not have a successful political career and resigned from public office in 1876 as a result of political scandals during Reconstruction. He died in Florida in 1933, the last surviving full-rank Civil War general.

Home of Great Writers and the Blues

> Long before I wrote stories, I listened for stories. Listening for them is something more acute than listening to them. When their elders sit and begin, children are just waiting and hoping for one to come out, like a mouse from its hole.
>
> — *Author Eudora Welty*, One Writer's Beginnings, *1984*

Mississippi offers a wealth of attractions to visitors. It is the home state of an amazing number of great musicians and writers. Artists as diverse as opera singer Leontyne Price and blues legend B. B. King were born in Mississippi. Many writers, among them Eudora Welty and William Faulkner, were born, lived, and died in the Magnolia State. Mississippi offers numerous attractions to people interested in history. Many mansions that belonged to plantation owners before the Civil War have been preserved and are now open to the public, and historic battlefields offer an opportunity to learn about the Civil War. Visitors to Mississippi today can learn about the state's cultural heritage and historic past while enjoying the wonderful music and food of this lovely state.

▼ **The Natchez Trace Trail travels from Nashville to Natchez. It was established by Native Americans and used for commerce from 1700 to 1890.**

Historic Sites

Mississippi is an ideal place to learn about the Civil War, as many battlefields have been preserved as historic sites. Vicksburg National Military Park commemorates one of the most important military campaigns of the Civil War, the siege of Vicksburg. The battlefield at Vicksburg has been preserved as it was at the time of the siege, along with a restored home of the period.

The Natchez Trace Parkway is a modern parkway planned to closely follow a route that has been traveled for hundreds of years. Native Americans had established this route before the arrival of the earliest European settlers. Today, the parkway runs for 444 miles (715 km) diagonally across the state from Natchez to Nashville, Tennessee.

In Natchez, visitors can get a glimpse of pre-Civil War life in the South as they tour restored mansions. Over five hundred of these homes remain intact, some of which have more than twenty rooms filled with antique furniture and chandeliers imported from Europe.

A visitor to Mississippi who is interested in the many writers and musicians born there can choose from several historic sites. Among them is Rowan Oak in Oxford, the home of Pulitzer Prize-winning novelist William Faulkner, who wrote several of his books there. Rowan Oak is now registered as a National Historic Landmark and maintained by the University of Mississippi. For fans of popular music, the birthplace of Elvis Presley in Tupelo is also open to the public as part of Elvis Presley Center.

Rosswood Plantation

In 1834, twenty-seven years before the start of the Civil War, Captain Isaac Ross freed his slaves in his will. Today, Rosswood Plantation, built by his grandson in 1857, stands on the site of the captain's home. Rosswood Plantation in Lorman is on the National Register of Historic Places. Visitors can tour this home and learn about the courageous man who turned against slavery decades before the rest of the South.

Museums and Libraries

Mississippi has a wealth of museums devoted to art, history, and music. The Mississippi Museum of Art in Jackson, the Mary Buie Museum in Oxford, and the Lauren Rogers Museum of Art in Laurel attract visitors with their collections of antique scientific instruments, Greek and Roman coins, and American art. The Mississippi Museum of Natural Science and the Mississippi State Historical Museum, both located in the state capital of Jackson, have permanent exhibits relating to the natural and social history of the state. The Delta Blues Museum in Clarksdale, located in a former railroad depot, houses exhibits about the culture and people of blues music. Visitors can view photos and read about the blues while listening to the music of Muddy Waters and Robert Johnson, two of its brightest stars.

Mississippi's first public library opened in 1818 in Port Gibson. The state now has about 250 public libraries. Several college and university libraries hold collections of interest for people researching Mississippi and its history. The University of Mississippi library houses an important

▲ Mississippi is considered the birthplace of the Blues. Clarksdale is home to the Delta Blues Museum. The Blues genre developed from the music and experiences of African Americans during slavery and afterward.

archive of William Faulkner's books, manuscripts, and papers. The most complete collection of historical documents in the state is housed in the Mississippi Department of Archives and History Library.

Communications

Twenty daily newspapers are published in the state. The daily newspaper with the largest circulation is the Jackson *Clarion-Ledger*, serving the capital city. Other important daily papers include the *Sun Herald* in Biloxi and the *Hattiesburg American*. The first newspapers published in Mississippi were the *Mississippi Gazette* (1800), the *Intelligencer* (1801), and the *Mississippi Herald* (1802). These newspapers were published in Natchez. The oldest newspaper still published in Mississippi is the *Woodville Republican*, founded in 1823.

Music and Theater

Known as the home of blues music and Elvis Presley, Mississippi also has many other forms of music and entertainment. Professional opera, ballet, and theater companies offer Mississippians and visitors a range of choices. Mississippi boasts two opera companies, Opera South and the

▼ The Mississippi Sports Hall of Fame and Museum in Jackson is dedicated to preserving and publicizing the achievements of sports figures associated with Mississippi.

Mississippi Opera Association. Opera South stages two major productions every year. The Mississippi Opera, founded in 1945, performs opera and offers workshops to local opera lovers. Numerous opera festivals in Mississippi provide both ticketed and free events. The Natchez Opera Festival was established in 1991 and has recently restored a theater for its productions.

Mississippi produced two of the greatest musicians of the twentieth century. William Grant Still, known as "the dean of African-American composers," combined classical musical styles of European origin with African-American music in a way that was completely original. Still was the first African American to conduct a major symphony orchestra, and his *Afro-American Symphony* was among the most popular symphonies of its time. Opera singer Leontyne Price made her Metropolitan Opera debut in 1961 in Verdi's *Il Trovatore* and thereafter sang leading roles in the great opera houses of the world. In 1964, Price was the first Mississippian to be awarded the Presidential Medal of Freedom.

Sports

Mississippi has a thriving college and university sports scene, with prominent football, basketball, and baseball teams. Sports fans in the Magnolia State have made the annual football game between the University of Mississippi (Oxford) Rebels and the Mississippi State (Starkville) Bulldogs the most popular sports event of the year. The Bulldogs have had outstanding seasons since 1990, playing in six football bowl games.

Mississippi has produced many great sports figures in the last century. Two brothers, Commodore and Roy Cochran, were the first siblings to win Olympic gold medals. These talented track and field athletes won a total

DID YOU KNOW?

Mississippi has several winning college teams. Among them are the Mississippi State Bulldogs, the University of Mississippi Rebels, and the Jackson State University Tigers. Mississippians have won national college championships in tennis, basketball, football, and soccer.

of three gold medals in the 1924 and 1948 games. Other Olympic athletes include Glen Hardin, who won silver and gold medals in the 1932 and 1936 games for the 400-meter hurdles, and Rowdy Gaines, who won a gold medal for the 100-meter freestyle swimming event in the 1984 games.

A baseball great also called Mississippi home as a boy. Jay Hanna "Dizzy" Dean spent much of his young life in Bond, Mississippi, honing the skills that would make him one of professional baseball's best-known pitchers. Dean helped the St. Louis Cardinals win the World Series in 1934 and later played for the Chicago Cubs. He retired from professional baseball in 1941 and began working as a television sports commentator in 1950. Dean was inducted into the Baseball Hall of Fame in 1953.

Two boxing legends hailed from Mississippi. Archie Moore, the world light-heavyweight champion from 1952 to 1962, was known for his fierce style in the ring. His fights ended in a record number of knockouts. Henry Armstrong, a native of Columbus, held the world featherweight champion title from 1937 to 1938, the world lightweight champion title in 1938, and the world welterweight champion title from 1938 to 1940. He is the only boxer ever to hold three world titles at the same time.

▶ Crawford, Mississippi, native Jerry Rice attended college at Mississippi Valley State in Itta Bena. Drafted in 1985 by the San Francisco 49ers, Rice has since accumulated fourteen NFL records, twelve Pro Bowl invitations, and three Super Bowl rings.

Mississippi Greats

Ralph Boston was one of the stars of the 1960 Olympics. Born in 1939, in Laurel, Boston studied at Tennessee A & I University and competed in numerous track and field events. Boston set a world record for the long jump of 26 feet, 11¼ inches (8.2m) in 1960, breaking the mark set by Jesse Owens twenty-five years before. It was the first of five world records Boston established in the event. He set his last world record in the long jump in May 1965, with a distance of 27 feet, 5 inches (8.4m).

Jerry Rice, born in 1962, is thought to be the greatest wide receiver ever to play in the National Football League. As a rookie with the San Francisco 49ers, Rice struggled to compete with the pros, but he soon came into his own and now ranks with other football legends like Charlie Taylor and Don Hutson.

Great Mississippians

When the last ding-dong of doom has clanged and faded from the last worthless rock hanging tideless in the last red and dying evening, . . . even then there will still be one more sound: that of his [man's] puny, inexhaustible voice, still talking.

— *Author William Faulkner, Nobel Prize acceptance speech, 1950*

Following are only a few of the thousands of people who were born, died, or spent much of their lives in Mississippi and made extraordinary contributions to the state and the nation.

WILLIAM FAULKNER
WRITER

BORN: *September 25, 1897, New Albany*
DIED: *July 6, 1962, Oxford*

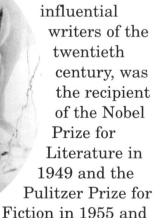

William Faulkner, widely considered one of the most influential writers of the twentieth century, was the recipient of the Nobel Prize for Literature in 1949 and the Pulitzer Prize for Fiction in 1955 and 1963. His novels, including *Absalom, Absalom!* and the groundbreaking *The Sound and the Fury,* are still widely read today.

RICHARD WRIGHT
WRITER

BORN: *September 4, 1908, near Natchez*
DIED: *November 28, 1960, Paris, France*

Richard Wright, the son of sharecroppers and the great-grandson of slaves, was the first African-American novelist to reach a wide audience in this country. His thirteen novels, *Black Boy*, *The Outsiders*, and *Native Son* among them, are considered classics. They describe the difficulties suffered by African Americans in the first half of the twentieth century. Wright quit school in the ninth grade and later worked for the post office in Chicago. Around this time, his first published work, a short story titled "Superstition," appeared. He became involved with black literary groups, began to write seriously, and eventually was hired by the Federal Writers Project to research the history of African Americans in the city of Chicago.

Wright's first novel, *Native Son*, published in 1940, was a successful Broadway play. The ongoing racial conflict in the United States caused Wright's move to Paris in the late 1940s.

EUDORA WELTY
WRITER

BORN: *April 13, 1909, Jackson*
DIED: *July 22, 2001, Jackson*

Eudora Welty lived almost her entire life in her parents' house in Jackson. After attending the University of Wisconsin and Columbia Business School in New York, Welty returned to Mississippi to write the novels and short stories that have assured her a place in history. From the comic short story, "Why I Live at the P.O." to the later novel *Losing Battles*, her ear for dialogue and keen eye for the details of southern life produced works that have pleased readers for over sixty years. She won the Pulitzer Prize for Fiction in 1969 for *The Optimist's Daughter* and the Presidential Medal of Freedom in 1980. Describing what some might call a sheltered life, Welty wrote, "A sheltered life can be a daring life as well. For all serious daring starts from within."

TENNESSEE WILLIAMS
WRITER

BORN: *March 26, 1911, Columbus*
DIED: *February 24, 1983, New York City*

Tennessee Williams's plays changed the course of the American theater. Williams published his first story, "The Vengeance of Nitocris," in *Weird Tales*, a popular magazine, at the age of seventeen. His first play, *Cairo, Shanghai, Bombay*, was produced in Memphis, Tennessee, in 1937. Williams gained international fame when his play *The Glass Menagerie* was produced on Broadway in 1945. Between 1945 and 1952, he had four other plays produced on Broadway: *A Streetcar Named Desire*, *Summer and Smoke*, *The Rose Tattoo*, and *Camino Real*. In all, Williams wrote sixty-five plays, two novels, sixty short stories, two books of poetry, numerous essays, and an autobiography. He received the Pulitzer Prize for Drama in 1945 and 1955, the Academy Award for Best Picture in 1958, and the Presidential Medal of Freedom in 1980.

SHELBY FOOTE
WRITER

BORN: *November 17, 1916, Greenville*

Shelby Foote, the great-grandson of a judge and the grandson of a state senator, grew up with a strong sense of his family's place in the history of the South. After studying at the University of North Carolina for two years, Foote joined the National Guard and eventually was made a captain, serving in Northern Ireland during World War II. Upon his return to the United States, Foote worked for the Associated Press and began writing seriously. His research on the great battles of the Civil War led to his novel, *Shiloh*, published in 1952. After writing five novels, Foote turned to nonfiction. His three-volume work, *The Civil War*, which took almost twenty years to complete, earned him a Pulitzer Prize nomination.

MEDGAR EVERS
CIVIL RIGHTS LEADER

BORN: *July 2, 1925, near Decatur*
DIED: *June 12, 1963, Jackson*

As the head of Mississippi's chapter of the NAACP, Medgar Evers fought for civil rights. After fighting in the Battle of Normandy with the U.S. Army in World War II and graduating from Alcorn State University, Evers began working for the NAACP, organizing boycotts of gas stations that refused to allow blacks to use their restrooms. Determined to gain equal rights for African Americans, Evers investigated violent crimes, organized more boycotts, and fought to force the University of Mississippi in Oxford to admit its first African-American student, James Meredith. Evers was assassinated by a white supremacist in 1963. After two jury trials ended in deadlocks, a third jury convicted Evers's killer and sentenced him to life in prison.

B. B. KING
BLUES MUSICIAN

BORN: *September 16, 1925, Itta Bena*

The great blues legend B. B. King, born Riley B. King on a cotton plantation, began his musical career playing the guitar on street corners for dimes. At the age of twenty-two, he hitchhiked to Memphis, Tennessee, to begin his musical career in earnest. Within a year, he was performing on a popular radio show and appearing in nightclubs. In 1951, King had the first of two number-one R&B (rhythm and blues) hits, "Three O'clock Blues," and began to tour the United States. Since then, King has never stopped touring, performing everywhere from symphony halls to small blues clubs. His unique guitar style, instantly recognizable to blues lovers, has earned him eight Grammy Awards. In 1987, King was inducted into the Rock and Roll Hall of Fame, and in 1990, he received the Presidential Medal of the Arts.

BO DIDDLEY
BLUES MUSICIAN

BORN: *December 30, 1928, McComb*

Bo Diddley, born Ellas Bates, first learned to play the violin, but switched to the guitar at age ten. As a young

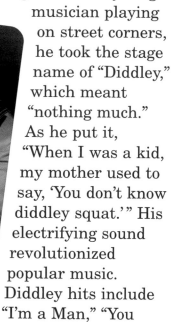

musician playing on street corners, he took the stage name of "Diddley," which meant "nothing much." As he put it, "When I was a kid, my mother used to say, 'You don't know diddley squat.'" His electrifying sound revolutionized popular music. Diddley hits include "I'm a Man," "You Can't Judge a Book by Its Cover," and "Shave and a Haircut." In 1987, Bo Diddley was inducted into the Rock and Roll Hall of Fame, and in 1998, he received a Grammy Award for lifetime achievement.

WILLIE MORRIS
WRITER AND EDITOR

BORN: *November 29, 1934, Jackson*
DIED: *August 2, 1999, Jackson*

Willie Morris, a sixth-generation Mississippian, was raised in a family of storytellers. At the University of Texas, as editor of the school newspaper, he angered school officials with his attacks on segregation. After studying at Oxford University in England as a Rhodes Scholar, Morris began working as a journalist. In 1967, he was made editor-in-chief of *Harper's* magazine, the youngest person ever to hold that position. That same year he published an autobiographical work, *North Towards Home*, about growing up in the South. In 1980, Morris was appointed writer-in-residence at the University of Mississippi. He continued to write about life in the South, including a book of essays, *Homecomings*, and the nonfiction work *The Ghosts of Medgar Evers*, about Medgar's assassination. Morris's work reflects a love of Mississippi and offers keen insight into how the South is different from the rest of the United States.

ELVIS PRESLEY
MUSICIAN

BORN: *January 8, 1935, Tupelo*
DIED: *August 16, 1977, Memphis, Tennessee*

Elvis Presley was raised in an extremely religious home. As a child, he sang in church choirs and began to develop the singing style that would appeal to teenagers (and simultaneously infuriate their parents) in the 1950s. After graduating from high school in 1953, Elvis made a private recording for his beloved mother Gladys. His soulful voice

caught the attention of a record producer, and a year later Elvis released his first record, "That's All Right, Mama." His appearance on a hit TV show of the era, *The Ed Sullivan Show,* cemented his status as a teenage rebel: His dancing, tame by today's standards, was considered so wild that the cameras were allowed to film him only from the waist up. Millions of records and thirty-three movies later, Elvis was a national phenomenon. He continued to perform until his drug-related death at the age of forty-two.

JIM HENSON
PUPPETEER AND PRODUCER

BORN: *September 24, 1936, Greenville*
DIED: *May 16, 1990, New York, NY*

Jim Henson was an artistic child who loved to paint and draw. He developed a style of puppet known as a "Muppet," part marionette, part puppet. At the age of nineteen, Henson had his own TV show starring a lovable frog named Kermit. After Kermit and Henson appeared on *The Tonight Show* in 1957, the Muppets grew in popularity. Jim Henson's biggest break came in 1969 when he worked on the *Sesame Street* show, creating characters such as Big Bird, Ernie, Bert, and the Cookie Monster. Later, Henson worked on other TV shows and movies such as *The Dark Crystal* and *Labyrinth*.

Mississippi
History At-A-Glance

1540
Hernando de Soto begins his exploration of the area now known as Mississippi.

1716
The second French settlement is founded at Fort Rosalie by Pierre Le Moyne's brother, Jean Baptiste.

1876
The Reconstruction era in Mississippi ends as Democrats gain control of the state legislature.

1699
The first settlement of the French colony is founded by Pierre Le Moyne, Sieur d'Iberville, at Ocean Springs.

1798
The Mississippi Territory is established.

1818
Mississippi's first public library opens in Port Gibson.

1861
Mississippi secedes from the Union.

1763
France loses its war with Great Britain. Great Britain wins the Mississippi region.

1817
Mississippi becomes a state.

1822
Jackson is named the state capital.

1863
Vicksburg is captured. The siege lasted six weeks.

1890
A new state constitution is adopted, effectively denying civil rights to African Americans.

1600   **1700**   **1800**

1492
Christopher Columbus comes to New World.

1607
Capt. John Smith and three ships land on Virginia coast and start first English settlement in New World — Jamestown.

1754–63
French and Indian War.

1776
Declaration of Independence adopted July 4.

1787
U.S. Constitution written.

1773
Boston Tea Party.

1777
Articles of Confederation adopted by Continental Congress.

1812–14
War of 1812.

United States
History At-A-Glance

1927
The Mississippi River floods, causing property damage and loss of life.

1936
In an effort to create jobs for Mississippians and stabilize the economy, the Balance Agriculture With Industry program is created.

1962
Author William Faulkner dies on July 6.

1962
The first African-American student is enrolled at the University of Mississippi. James Meredith graduated from the university in 1963.

1963
Medgar Evers is assassinated.

1969
Charles Evers, Medgar's brother, is elected mayor of Fayette.

1969
A federal court orders Mississippi to desegregate its schools.

1980
Tennessee Williams is awarded the Presidential Medal of Freedom.

1987
Lawmakers vote to build a new four-lane highway system.

1992
Kirk Fordice is elected governor.

2000
Unemployment falls to 5.7 percent.

2001
Eudora Welty dies on July 22.

1800	1900	2000

1848
Gold discovered in California draws eighty thousand prospectors in the 1849 Gold Rush.

1861–65
Civil War.

1869
Transcontinental railroad completed.

1917–18
U.S. involvement in World War I.

1929
Stock market crash ushers in Great Depression.

1941–45
U.S. involvement in World War II.

1950–53
U.S. fights in the Korean War.

1964–73
U.S. involvement in Vietnam War.

2000
George W. Bush wins the closest presidential election in history.

2001
A terrorist attack in which four hijacked airliners crash into New York City's World Trade Center, the Pentagon, and farmland in western Pennsylvania leaves thousands dead or injured.

▼ Cotton pickers at work in a Mississippi field about 1885.

Festivals and Fun for All

Check web site for exact date and directions.

Natchez Fall Pilgrimage, Natchez

Journey to Natchez in October during the Fall Pilgrimage to listen to music, tour historic houses, and eat traditional Southern food.

www.natchezpilgrimage.com

Black History Month, Natchez

This February event in Natchez celebrates the proud history of African Americans in Mississippi.

www.natchez.ms.us

Carnival Association of Long Beach Mardi Gras and Parade, Long Beach

Celebrate Mardi Gras in this beautiful beach town. All the traditional trappings of the event are here — beads, glitter, and outdoor excitement.

www.longbeachcarnival.com

The Elvis Presley Festival, Tupelo

Celebrate the life of the king of rock and roll in his hometown at this June festival featuring the music that influenced Elvis.

www.tupeloelvisfestival.com

Highway 61 Blues Festival, Leland

This June festival celebrates the classic Mississippi blues born on the Delta.

www.highway61blues.nstemp.com

The Howlin' Wolf Memorial Blues Festival, West Point

This lively blues festival is held in August in the hometown of Chester Arthur Burnett, known as Howlin' Wolf.

www.wpnet.org

The Miss Mississippi Parade, Vicksburg

Marching bands, drill teams, and a parade featuring all of the Miss Mississippi contestants are highlights of this summer weekend festival.

www.vicksburgcvb.org

Mississippi Delta Blues and Heritage Festival, Greenville

Held each September, this exciting festival features blues music, red beans and rice, fried catfish, and arts and crafts.

www.deltablues.org

Spring Festival and Barbecue Cook-Off, Southhaven

You'll find music and plenty of prize-winning barbecued food at this down-home Mississippi festival held each April.

www.desotonet.com/
cityofsouthaven/springfest.htm

Natchez Opera Festival, Natchez

Listen to great opera and visit the antebellum mansions of this historic town during this exciting spring festival in the home state of opera great Leontyne Price.

www.alcorn.edu/opera/

Okeelala Festival, Baldwyn

Come to Baldwyn in October for an antique car show, amusement park rides, and live entertainment all day.

www.baldwyn.ms/fest.htm

The Southern Farm Bureau Golf Classic, Madison

Gather together with the crowds at this October PGA golf tournament at the Annandale Golf Club in Madison. Golf lovers have attended this tournament since 1968.

www.pgatour.com/tournaments/r054

World Catfish Festival, Belzoni

At this April festival, you can help crown the Catfish Queen, enjoy the world's largest fish fry, and then participate in a catfish-eating contest.

www.catfishcapitalonline.com

Yazoo County Holiday Parade, Yazoo City

Celebrate the winter holidays with floats, bands, and home-cooked food at this classic southern fair.

www.yazoo.org/CalEvent.htm

▶ Since the King of Rock and Roll died in 1977, more than 100,000 Elvis fans visit his birthplace in Tupelo each year.

Books

Coleman, Evelyn. *The Riches of Oseola McCarty*. Chicago: Albert Whitman, 1998. After working all her life, Oseola McCarty decided to leave her life savings, a large sum of money, to start a scholarship at the University of Southern Mississippi.

Coulter, Tony. *La Salle and the Explorers of the Mississippi*. Broomall, PA: Chelsea House, 1991. A nonfiction account of one of the first explorers of the Mississippi River.

Harness, Cheryl. *Mark Twain and the Queens of the Mississippi*. New York: Simon and Schuster, 1998. A richly illustrated and informative account of Mark Twain and his work as an apprentice steamboat captain on the Mississippi River.

Lourie, Peter. *Mississippi River: A Journey Down the Father of Waters*. Sherman, CT: Boyd Mills Press, 2000. A firsthand account of a trip down the Mississippi River, with photos by the author.

Meigs, Cornelia. *Swift Rivers*. Cambridge, MA: Walker, 1994. In this Newbery Honor Roll novel, a young man floats down the Mississippi and meets raft hands and river pilots along the way.

Web Sites

▶ Official state web site
www.ms.gov

▶ City of Jackson homepage
www.city.jackson.ms.us

▶ Mississippi Department of Archives and History
www.mdah.state.ms.us

▶ Mississippi Historical Society
mshistory.k12.ms.us